ANCHOR
BOOKS

MAKE A WISH VOL II . . .
MOONBEAMS IN A JAR

Edited by

Neil Day

First published in Great Britain in 2001 by
ANCHOR BOOKS
Remus House,
Coltsfoot Drive,
Peterborough, PE2 9JX
Telephone (01733) 898102

HB ISBN 1 85930 940 2
SB ISBN 1 85930 945 3

FOREWORD

Moonbeams In A Jar is a unique anthology depicting the wishes and desires of not only ourselves but also the people around us.

This Anchor Books publication was put together in recognition of Make-A-Wish Foundation® UK's annual national awareness campaign in January 2001.

Poets from far and wide have come together and allowed us to share with them their ultimate wishes, whether it be a longing for world peace or the desire to reach their ultimate goal.

Make-A-Wish Foundation® UK has one very simple objective - to grant the favourite wishes of children aged between three and eighteen suffering from life-threatening illnesses.

Moonbeams In A Jar will not only be a popular read for all who come across it but it will give us the chance to help these children have their wishes come true.

Neil Day
Editor

CONTENTS

UNTITLED

If you made a wish, what would it be?
Perhaps that all the blind would see,
Or to never again know any fear,
Or maybe that the deaf would hear?

If you made a wish, what would it be?
Never to know illness again maybe?
To never lose loved ones? - They'd never die
To never scream 'Why God, why?'

If you made a wish, what would it be?
To get out of your wheelchair and simply run free,
Put an end to suffering, pain and sorrow,
To know you'll be cured come tomorrow?

If I could wish for just one thing
I'd never fear what tomorrow would bring.

I wish life wasn't so unfair
I wish that there was no despair
I wish these diseases didn't exist
There are so many things on my list.

Dorothy Watkins

HOPEFULNESS

I wish that I was a bird
So that I could soar on high
But that would be absurd
As I don't have wings to fly.

I wish I was a fish
So I could swim the oceans deep
But that would be a silly wish
As where would I go to sleep?

I wish I was a lioness
The pride of the open plain
But that wish too is useless
I no longer have a flowing mane!

I had a hundred and one wishes
As I lay there in my bed
Being spoon fed from plastic dishes
Bandages covering my face and head.

I wished the driver of the other car
Had not had so much to drink
I wished he'd not gone into the bar
But I guess he didn't think.

I lay there in the hospital
Another statistic on the books
And I wished for the near impossible
That surgeons could restore my looks.

Don't set your sights too high
That's my advice to you
But don't let dreams fade and die
Wishes really can come true.

My wish came true eventually
My dreams hopefully, all fulfilled
As I wished peace also for the family
Of the driver who was killed!

Gwyneth Wynn-Davies

I WISH I WAS A CLOWN
(Dedicated to Genna)

Every year the circus comes to town
I wish I could be a clown.

I'd wear Dad's Doc Martin boots
With extra long laces

Paint two tears upon my face

I'll prance and dance around the ring
Act really crazy, do my own thing

Pretend my water pistol's a shooter
then drive my trick banger car
while papping its klaxston hooter

Then when it's all blown apart
I'll run and jump on my scooter

While riding around exciting the crowd
they'll never guess it's me.

The kids laugh and clap so loud
As I squirt my water pistol into the crowd

Most kids laugh but some do cry
Suddenly I'm awake with a tear in my eye

As I leave the ring and wave them goodbye

One day my wish will come true
And I will be a clown in the circus too.

Graham Hare

MY CHILDREN

My wish for both girl and boy
Not glory, fortune or great wealth
But that you know love and joy
And through your life enjoy good health
And always care for one another
At home, abroad in foreign climes
Just think and act just like your mother
Who was your guardian at all times.
This is my wish and if it's granted
Will be enough and all that's wanted.

J Campbell

. . . WISHERS . . .

Fly on moonbeams of mind, then sail the Cosmos in spirit,
We are star chasers, dreamers all,
and so we behold the true human soul . . .
Far can we travel, by our dreams power we race.
Through ceaseless depths of time,
across endless seas of space.
Our eyes see all Earth's beauty, through the majesty
of imagination, free . . .
Our minds talk with God in silent whispers,
telepathic radiating heavenbound.
With dreams and the rising and falling of a star,
at each new day's moments dawning . . .
Glowing within, with star-fire light, an inner
all-pervading presence . . .
Our souls are free souls of love and liberty,
that quest always for the eternal force
that bade creation.
Upon a magical odyssey through worlds beyond -
then we return to our home, this living Earth . . .
Blue and shining, with life's abundance,
against the jade, ever night, all about . . .
Quenched by the stars, fed by their power,
filled with infinite forces,
we become earthbound once more . . .
Into dreaming sleep; human realm,
and recall the adventure . . .
Our soul's quest that's starbound, which twinkles
just beginning in all our hearts' wishes . . .

P Holland

ANGELS SINGING

Dancing around the Christmas tree,
There's nowhere else I'd rather be.
Open presents on the floor,
You got me just what I adore.
Mummy said that it's for me,
She got one for the whole family.
Open yours quick, I know you'll like it,
It's the one you saw when we got your jacket.
Come with me, please, to see the angel,
She's sitting high up on the tree.
She's my favourite part of Christmas,
Mummy said she'll always be with me.
Hear the angels singing loud,
There sitting just there on a cloud.
When I'm sitting up there with them,
Will you sing along with me.

Anne Rickard

WISH FULFILMENT

I wish I had the wings of a wild swan.
First I would skim lake water, then be gone.
I would stretch out my neck, fly under a cloud.
Ever stately - not gawky, honking loud
Like some of the geese of my acquaintance.
Be sure I won't favour them with a glance -
As high over a northern sea I fly
Where bluish-white icebergs come floating by . . .

But no - I'm still myself. I cannot fly.
To leave this Earth even swans cannot try.
I'll take myself off in the next rocket,
Not to moon or Mars, but a far planet
At the other side of the Milky Way
Where winged beings live, so the experts say.
Whoosh! I'm *off!* Sound like a shot from a gun
. . . Many light years away from our own sun.

Rocket crash-lands. Write-off. No return to Earth.
A wingless human arouses much mirth.
Aliens graft on me such splendid wings.
I'll soon forget most Earth-limiting things.
No need here for car, taxi, bus or train,
Now I have become my own aeroplane!
I hover, look down on sea, turquoise-blue,
The rest of this planet beautiful too.

C Creedon

A WISH FOR THE WORLD

To have all that we need
Is all that I wish for.
Need does not call for greed
So there'd be no more war.
Want, would be forgotten
We would be all sharing.
For the few who sicken
There would be deep caring.
Yes, to have all we need
Is all I'm wishing for.

C A Satterthwaite

THREE WISHES

Wish, wish, wish, if only I had been a fish
I could have swum the ocean wide,
Atlantic and Pacific, had I only been a fish,
but then again I could be baked and end up in a dish.

Wish, wish, wish, if I hadn't been a fish
a leopard I could be
chasing game for dinner, how my tail would swish
but then I could end up a rug, I'd rather be a fish.

Wish, wish, wish, if I couldn't be a fish,
I'd like to be an Arctic tern.
Fly down to cold Antarctica and, back again on fish,
caught in the sea on wing, I'm glad I'm not a fish.

I've had three wishes three times o'er,
I've flown and swum, run free,
can't think of any other thing or person I would be,
so I might as well forget the wishes, just be glad I'm me.

Derek B Hewertson

THE WISH I HAVE IN ME

It may seem strange
But yet it's true,
The wish I have in me
To plant a tree and see it grow,
I've had it since I was a boy,
But some things take a time to show,
And now's the time to start.
I've seen Nature starting on her own,
A young pine tree from the cone.
A stripling oak, an ash half-grown.
I'd like to see a tree grown tall,
Planted by me, and feel I'd had a part,
However small, in the wonder of it all.

Stewart Gordon

TO BE NOTICED

I wish that he could see me
I'm sure he'd like my smile
If only he would take the time
To sit and talk awhile
He'd listen to my gentle voice
He'd see these sparkly eyes
I'm sure he'll think I'm funny,
Maybe, even nice.
I watch him as he passes by
I raise my hand to wave
But off he goes without a glance
Another life to save
I know I'm being selfish
When all he does is good
But how I wish, I really wish,
I really wish he would.

Susan Stark

I Wish

I wish for general world progress
I wish for the day
Through science we know the reason why
For the day when there are no diseases
Instead money and time can be applied to preventive measures
I wish for ethical medical progress
For child and animal exploitation to cease
I wish for the criminal laws to be reviewed
So that human life has a higher value
For the human race to continue to keep their own self respect
So in turn continue to respect their fellow comrades
I wish for man to stop world irony
So the world's races could perhaps live in rapport and harmony.

Mary Wood

WISHES

Wishes are like stars, they shine on you
Do they come true? I'm sure they do.
Wishes for happiness, some for love,
Come showered like sunbeams from above.
But in my heart my wish I pray,
Will come true for me one day.

Christine Munton

WISHFUL THINKING

What I lack in life's a name
One that would conjure up!
Wealth, security and fame
To make them all look up.

Like Hercules, and Pericles,
And other names as sound.
As those men in history
Whose names are so renowned.

But all these names I cannot use
For they are second-hand
And if I could, what hopes have I
To reach the heights where now they stand.

Then whilst in dream I realised
My searchings were in vain
For it's not the name which makes the man
But the man, who makes the name!

A P Hollick

WHAT IS YOUR WISH?

What is your wish?
I wish for freedom.
What is your wish?
I wish for peace.
What is your wish?
I wish for happiness.
What is your wish?
I wish for love.
What is your wish?
I wish for success.
What is your wish?
I wish for you!

Samantha Allerston (18)

DELICATESSEN

I wish
For a dish
Of my favourite recipe,
With long dark hair,
And stirring eyes at me,
With a touch of spice
Of a bare left shoulder,
That would entice
Me to stare
As I watch her smoulder,
And serve her up as a tasty meal,
To feast my eyes
On her culinary appeal.

Anthony John Ward

I WISH

I wish for care and tenderness,
To spread across our lands,
For evil to be eaten up,
So all God's creatures,
Can live life safely,
Side by side,
With this fellow man.

I wish for,
For fresh air,
The simple things,
So we can all attune,
Look closer at the natural,
Not all doom and gloom.

The natural is beautiful,
Through all it has a spark,
It takes away the shadows,
Opens up our hearts.

This all can be achieved,
Eventually it can.
Giving, not taking,
The free will,
Of the dedicated man.

J B Beaumont

I WISH, I WISH, I WISH . . .

Life was flying by me,
I didn't understand it,
I think my life is worthless,
Time is ticking away,
People don't understand me,
What can I do?
Make a wish, make a wish, make a wish!

Sharon Hughes

IF I COULD TURN BACK TIME

If I could turn back time
play through fields of golden grain
Follow the lapwing, watch the lark
Sail paper boats till almost dark.

If I could turn back time
With sandals on my feet
Red ribbons in my hair
brown weather-beaten cheeks.
Walk the laneways where
Honeysuckle grows, gather primroses
Till evening dew dampens my feet.

If I could turn back time,
Wishful thinking that can never be
I sit here wondering
What the future holds for me
Greatest principle in life is
Heaven for eternity.
A free gift, a perfect gift
Brothers and sisters rejoicing
In heavenly harmony.

Frances Gibson

A HOPEFUL WISH

A wish is something that you hope
will one day turn out true,
You can wish for anything you like,
it's really up to you.
If you are in hospital
the greatest wish you'll make!
Is that you'll soon get better, now that is no mistake.
Your closest friends and family
will visit you each day,
And help to keep you cheerful
No matter, come what may.
There may have been unpleasant things
that you've had to endure,
Which will all have been worthwhile
when you have a final cure.
So have faith in the doctors
and nurses on the ward,
And soon you'll be receiving
your true and just reward.
Thanks will be forthcoming
from everyone you love,
But there's someone
you must not forget,
Our good Lord up above.

Frank William Beever

MOTHER

I'm still mothered as a child should be,
I'm still cared for,
And brought up with the right morals.
Yet I'm a mother too now,
And trying so hard to provide,
The security and strength,
I have known and still know now.
She is my life and everything I do,
I do try to make it the best for her.
And in the not so distant future,
I will provide more than love and security
But the life I had when I was young.

Claire Sanderson

WISHES

Wish a smile.
Wish each mile.
Filled with happiness.
Wish a day.
Wish a night.
Nothing more or less.
Wish a sun.
Wish a moon.
Wish a joyful quest.
Wish for all who suffer.
Nothing but the best.

Wish a sunrise.
Wish a sunset.
Wish with all your heart.
Wish for joy.
Wish sadness never.
Make today your start.
Wish a song.
Wish a choir.
Wish a miracle or two.
Wish a rainbow.
Wish a shower.
Wish dreams that all come true.

Leslie F Higgins

ARTISTIC DESIRE

I wish I had a real artistic skill
So I could paint a picture with deft strokes.
I would approach my canvas with a will
And with my oils and palette depict folks.

My brush strokes would reveal their inner fears
Whilst capturing the child's mischievous smile
Or showing cause for a fond mother's tears
And loneliness of aged and senile.

Perhaps only in a truly visual form
Will comprehension mean something to me
For tattered clothes don't keep a body warm,
Appreciating grief needs empathy.

Artists depict what, in real life, is true.
Painting encapsulates their point of view.

John W Skepper

WISHING

This could be the day when you come back
So I brush my hair.
I am not careless in my dress.
I dust the room
I sweep the floor
My endless love for you,
Still asks for more.
I refresh flowers that are in my living room.
I bake a cake.
For all in all
There's still a chance that you could call,
I still do it, after all this time!
Tell myself, he'll come back today.
I was not idle in my waiting game.
I married, had a child,
For life goes on,
Other lips comfort anguish that the
Lonely can feel
For though I thought I'd died inside
When you had gone
I lived on,
But still my inner, inner heart
Continues to say,
That this could be the day.

Doreen Brook

SENSIBLE GIFTS

To smell the flowers, or newly-mown hay,
what lovelier scents than these,
and smell of newly-washed clothing
blowing in the breeze?

To see the smile that greets you,
like a flag unfurled,
sending its message far and wide,
brightening up the world.

To hear the ripple of a stream,
the wind tickling the trees.
The songs of birds, a baby's cry,
what sweeter sounds than these?

To taste the pleasure of a kiss from parent,
friend or lover.
To let you know that people care through
fair or rainy weather.

To touch and hold a dear one's hand and
gently show each day,
your hands and theirs will join and guide
each other on life's way.

Five precious gifts so freely given,
do we know their worth?
Touch, taste, smell, to see and hear,
what greater riches on earth.

Mary Heppenstall

HELPLESS

I lie in bed,
My body spent.

They care
About my despair
And I care
About their intent.

They give,
I take,
I sleep,
I wake,
I do not give.

My body is in bed,
My soul is not yet spent.

I do still live,
I can still give.

I can still love,
I can still care
And make their care worthwhile.

I can still smile.

If I can't cope
I can still hope.

Kate Laity

No More Regrets

No longer am I slave
to sentimental dreams
when in the heart of night
hot tears I shed,
and restless waited
for the dawn to break
through yet another day
filled with regret.

Helen Weatherby

DO WISHES COME TRUE?

Do wishes really come true?
If you wish hard enough they do
I wish the world as it was
When life was slow
When you could wander anywhere
And people said hello
I wish for pits to work again
See the big old pit wheel
I know that could come true
It could be for real.
Bring old picture houses back
Ice-cream with a wooden spoon
Bring back the horse and carriage
And long warm days in June
We can make the world how it was
We can all live in peace
If we all pulled together
All the bad things would cease
I've always dreamed of going
Back in time where I belong
Where I'm safe with all my family
To me that could never be wrong
But that wish can't come true
But I can live it all the same
With my family by my side
And our good old family name
Will it ever come true
Me and my family are living that way
Who knows maybe it will catch on
I look forward to that day

Lucy Lee

DREAMS OF THE WEST

Why when I sit with my thoughts all alone
Do I feel that the west coast is calling me home?
For I'd gladly step back forty years to be free
With my peat fire for warmth and a wick just to see
Bound by the pressures of town life demands
See my dream from afar for to dream's all I can
Yet at times as I think in the distance I hear
A west wind that cries me a yearning to near
But someday I know I will call it my home
With just valleys and mountains and shorelines to roam
Just the sounds of the wildlife and nature to please
As their beauty blows by on the wisp of a breeze
And with no better thoughts as I smile at the view
Is a life where it seems that my dreams have come true.

Ken Watson

HIGH RISE

If I could wish,
A wish to come true,
I would wish
for a vast sky of blue,
to watch from my window,
Way up high.

I would wish
for storm clouds
menacing and black,
crashing thunder and lightning crack,
to watch from my window,
Way up high.

I would wish,
for wispy white clouds,
to float like angels
with heraldic sounds,
to watch from my window,
Way up high.

I would wish,
for skies of fiery orange
and blazing red,
to watch from my window,
in my hospital bed,
this is my wish
if there's one to be had.

Anne Bruce

PARADISE

Is this what you seek.
Does your mind speak.
To come in marriage
Private telepathy
Your horse and carriage.

Ergo and Eros
Troy; the sultans
Dire Straits
Love comes now.

No entry destroyed
Mind not void
Nights in white satin
Never reaching the end
Just what you want to be
You'll be in the end.

Joyride.

Andrew Howarth

A SIMPLE WISH

I have one simple wish I hope to God will come true,
It concerns a little boy with an angel's smile and big eyes
of forget-me-not blue.
I wish him every happiness that a childhood can hold.
I wish him to run and laugh, to make trouble and be bold.
I wish I could give him the freedom other children take for granted,
I wish I could take away the burden for which he is always branded,
I wish I could let him know how much he means to us all.
I wish I could protect him from every harsh word or painful fall,
It's just a simple wish but what else can I do?
I've said my bit, God, now it's up to you.

Eileen Connors (17)

UNTITLED

To have one wish that could come true,
May not seem much to me and you,
A smile that lasts, that look of joy,
Upon the face of a girl or boy.
The pain beneath no one can feel,
A little fun may help to heal.
For just one day, we're all the same,
And the wish for them at long last came.

Michelle Carr

I WISH I WERE TALLER

I wish I were taller
Then I could see
Past a crowd standing in front of me
I could see in the mirror
I could see past a queue
Tall people
If only they knew
To be small,
Too small for the rides
People pushing past you
Pushing you aside
I hate being small
I want to be tall,
I really don't understand
Everyone else is bigger than me
Maybe they come from growing land!

Laura Hewitt (11)

FOREVER YOUNG

I really wish now I'm getting old that I felt the same inside
I don't, I feel forever young, then I look in the mirror and sigh
I really wish now I'm getting old people still laughed at my jokes
But they look at me with sympathy and I feel like such a dope.
I really wish, now I'm getting old, I could wear my teeth. It's sad.
I put them in and they pop out and end up in my bag.
Now I don't let it get to me, that would be a sin
I take my teeth out of my bag and I'm sure to get a grin.
Now getting old is not so bad when you feel forever young
With the man I love and my family, my wish for them is the *sun*.

Yvonne Magill

UNTITLED

The wish of a fish
As it splashes
And it swishes,
It dives
And it delves
Through the waves
On the water
Where its fins flap.
It swims
Over greens growing;
Seaweed,
And it shines,
Shimmering.
Reflected on the blue
And the hue
Of the water.
As it glides
And it slides
Through the waves
With the warmth
Of the sun
Giving light,
Colours bright,
Waters clear.
Oh, the wish of a fish,
Or the fish of a wish;
To wish to be a fish.

Lucy Trevitt

WISHES AT PEN-Y-FAN

I stared up into the stark majesty of Pen-Y-Fan, her summit a shining
jewel in the bright sunlight.
Oh! I wish to be up there, to make the climb, steep slopes, up and up
over Corn Du and on -

     To achieve
Come on then! *Go,* the effort make, your wish attain, walk and climb,
strain till every fibre of your being groans, and the heart now pulsing
with desire throbs with fulfilment.

     My wish achieved.
I stood on that stark peak, bare rocks shouldering their way through
sparse grass, cold winds chilling my heated flesh, mist clouds
menacing, threatening to obscure the view.

     I looked.
The steep slope down away through the stunted trees, waterfalls adding
a mist spray to the already damp air, and the lush green valley wherein
our camp site lay. Gentle stream, sheltering trees, warm atmosphere,
peace and rest.

     I wished.
Cwn Llwych, to lie in the comfort of your peaceful breast.

     I mused.
We struggle to reach the mountain top, position, power, authority,
riches, we attain, and then we envy, envy those we have surpassed, their
easy-going way of life, the freedom from stress, worry and must have.

     I wish.
To be content with what may come, if called to the mountain top, strive
with all my might, if to the valleys rest and be thankful.

     I pray.
That where God sends me there I shall serve and be content.

Alan Ellsmore

WORLD WISH ONE

I have one wish,
Of world peace and freedom;
The ability to walk without death
As a shadow hanging over our heads.
The right to sleep under a roof
With warm faces and food.
The due to work and survive
To earn and provide.
The choice to elect and select
To use words not effects.
The liberty to worship whom we choose,
Not to love and to lose.
The decision to talk without fire,
To discuss without lies.
The option to live, accept and let live,
To understand and to give.

Helen Marshall

WISHES

As I hold you close to me
I'll make a wish for you to see
For go, we will in shimmering light
To swim with dolphins through the night.
And in the morning you will find
Tranquillity, peace - and ease of mind
With your hand in mine.
Through blue waters glide
These gentle creatures heal your mind.

You touch but maybe not to see
A magic felt by you and me
My wish will come true
For your pain to ease
The dolphins are here aiming to please.

With contentment of mind
Hands reach out to hold
They understand the play involved
For so many children need to be
Helped by this valued therapy.

With prayer on my lips I watched and I wait
I look in your eyes and know you are safe
Revealing a new and tranquil scene
The dolphins have powers as yet unforeseen
But now as I look a change will take place
And you say your first word with a smile on your face.

Now it's time to go home from this beautiful place
Where dolphins glide with angelic grace
A power so strong - unseen by man
To feel God's presence I take your hand
My wish has come true for me and for you.

And as I listen those plaintive cries
Seem to penetrate my contentment of mind
I close my eyes as once again
That journey we took I knew I could find
A pleasure for you to weave in your dreams
And you swim with the dolphins
Once more it would seem
The world can find answers
To wishes we make
For someone we love and cannot forsake.

Irene Siviour

UNTITLED

One day I wished that I could be
having lots of cuddles from my friend Mickey.
With Donald, Pluto and Goofy as well,
all brought to life by the Disney spell.

I wish my wish would really come true,
but how will I get there? What can I do?
They're so far away, I fear it seems
I can only cuddle them when they're in my dreams.

But dreams come true sometimes I know,
and one day soon maybe I can go
To have those cuddles and laugh and sing,
and feel the magic only Disney can bring.

To give them a kiss and have a photo too,
is what I really long to do.
My fears and pains may seem to vanish,
And all because I made a wish.

William Edward Avery

A Wish For Today

If I could make
A wish for today on Earth
A little longer,
We all could stay.
To forbid all blood sport
Because animals should never
suffer in this cruel way.
Let nature prepare
all sick children
A most beautiful day
To heal their pain
And help them to play.
And if we could all give
A little more of our time,
To listen to the people
Who commit a crime,
Then living on Earth
Could be more divine.

J Weatherhead

WISHES

I wish I'd been an actor
I wish I'd been a saint
I wish I'd been an artist
Up to my bum in paint

I wish I'd been a surgeon
Or a comedian who's funny
I wish I'd been a millionaire
Up to my neck in money

I wish I'd been a builder
Or a miner down the pit
But I work repairing sewerage pipes
Up to my neck in mess!

Kevin Cooper

I WISH

I wish I was a superstar,
I wish I was a millionaire,
I wish I was a wrestler,
I wish I was a bear.

I wish I was an actor,
So that I could wear wigs,
I wish I was an astronaut
I wish I was Ryan Giggs.

I wish I was a king,
So that I could rule the land,
I wish I was an emperor
I wish I was a one-man band.

I wish I was a famous poet,
I wish I lived on the moon,
I wish I could travel the world,
In a hot air balloon!

I wish I was a clown,
With a red nose and a cheesy grin,
I wish I was a good boy,
So lots of merits I would win.

I wish I was a racing driver,
I wish I was a spy,
I wish I was invisible,
I wish that I could fly.

Although all these things,
I wish I could be,
I am just as happy being me.

Paul Guthrie

I WISH I HAD SECOND SIGHT

I wish I had second sight
to see invisible fights.
I could spot the fighting of a knight
and defeat the king's plight.
If only I had second sight . . .
I would be able to see a kite's flight.
I could see a dog's bite
and protect the victim from fright
if only I had second sight . . .
I could defeat my highest frights.
I would be able to see tiny mites
I wish I had second sight!

Robbie Pearson

GIFT WISH HORSES

If wishes were horses
My gifts would be
Three dun ponies with sharp ears
Two round bay cobs
Five long striding eventers
Seven racing thoroughbreds
Twelve unusually coloured unicorns
And one mild eyed grey on rockers.

Helen Thompson

CHOSEN WISH

I wished many times as a child,
Of that which I never had,
And as to why my wishes, never ever came true,
I often wondered,
And at times, it made me sad.

But now as I recall, those wishes I once made,
I have many happy memories of my childhood,
And the sadness, I once knew, now no longer exists
For happiness, is the one, with whom I am blessed.

So if I could have one wish,
It would be for all others, to be as fortunate as me,
- Just the same -
And whilst not always receiving
Everything which they wish for,
- Just like me -
That they too, may then happiness gain.

Bakewell Burt

A SECRET KNOWN BY ONLY YOU

A wish is something special
(A secret) known by only you
It's there when you feel down
Giving hope when you are blue
Children, in all innocence
Believe their young lives through
That the star they wish upon
Will make their dreams come true
Taking them to places
Where they'll meet kings and queens
Fantasy becomes reality
When you're granted all your dreams
A wish, a silent yearning
Held dear and never told
A silver thread we cling to
When our world is grey and cold!

Karl Jakobsen

SECOND CHANCE

I wish that I could take away the years
Which score old faces with the lines of pain,
That youth and beauty once so gloriously theirs
Could by some act of God be theirs again.

Once they were like me, the ancient ones,
With passion and purpose for the life ahead,
Who now despair and live with loneliness
Since most of their contemporaries are dead.

Why do we waste the endless hours of youth
When all too soon we too must join the old?
Why do we not clasp living with both hands
Before the burning flame of life grows cold?

I wish for the sake of millions yet to be
That every soul should have a second chance
To return to youth with life's experience
And banish old age without a second glance.

Pamela Constantine

PEACE OF MIND

I wish, how I wish, for peace of mind.
For tranquillity and contentment.
To know that bitterness and hurt have gone for good,
though the loneliness will never cease.
To hope for dignity and understanding when feelings of
worthlessness abound.
I wish, how I wish, for peace of mind.

Ann Allen

WISHES

I wish I was a kitten
Always sleeping and playing
Drinking cream milk in kitchen
Then whereto and not saying.

I wish I was a big bird
Flying to sea and then rest
Meeting birds just to be heard
At night safely in my nest.

I wish I was a puppy
Waggling my tail all day
Always playful and happy
Then deepest sleep I'm away.

Thinking now what ought to be
Birthdays without a present
Christmas without any tree
Gifts are always to me sent.

Always my life just the same
Without mum and dad whereto
Life is much more than a game
Without parents what to do.

Peter Arthur Butcher

I WISH YOU LOVE

I see you, and wish I could talk to you
I wish I could tell you how I feel,
How much I love you, want you
How much I wish you loved me too,
I see the hurt in your eyes
I wish I could take the pain away,
She's walking all over you, I see that
I wish I could find the words I need to say.
I saw the bruises when you suffered
I wish I could kiss them all away
I wish I knew your reasons
For the price you're having to pay.
I wish I was the one you came home to
I wish I was the one in your heart,
I know you deserve to be happy
But I wish we could make a new start.
I wish, every day, every minute
As I write this, there's a wish in each line
I wish you peace, love and happiness
Most of all though, I wish you were mine.

Margaret Ann Scott

WHEN YOU WERE TWO

I look at the photos and
I wish for the summer
When you were two
Your hair bleached blonde stripes
Your smocked yellow sundress
Showed your shoulders, arms and elbows
You were delicious
You were talking in sentences
I couldn't believe it.

We went to the cake shop
And each time you chose the same
A doughnut
'With hundreds and thousands on it'.
I couldn't believe the joy
Walking slowly in the sunshine
Holding a tiny warm hand
Leaning slightly to reach it.

I watched as your pale white skin
Became a little more sun-tinged each day
I thought
She will never be prettier
We will never be anything
Like this again.

Denise Lee

A WISH I KNOW WILL COME TRUE

I am blind and cannot read or write,
I pray to the Lord, to give me back my sight,
Then I can both read and write,
And help others in the same plight,
To strengthen my Faith day by day,
Knowing my wish is on its way.

I know if the skies are always blue,
It seems my dreams are coming true,
And when the flowers bloom in the spring,
That's when my luck really begins,
And if I can smile when things go wrong,
And then I know I'm really on song.

Jan Graver-Wild

A WISH FOR MY DAUGHTER

I wish to my daughter to give
The wedding she'll never forget,
On the breadline as I do live
Overspent and full of regret.

A wonderful man she has met
A farmer who has brightened her life,
They met by chance on the 'net
And now he wants her to be his wife.

She's a daughter who's really a peach
Her happiness I have to endorse,
She wants to wed her man on a beach
Somewhere hot overseas of course.

She's a daughter with a beautiful smile
Always giving, not one to complain,
Although her wedding she's put off for a while
I know it is causing her pain.

I'm a mother who has let her down bad
Not having money banked in reserve,
So I wish for the chance to be had
And give the wedding she'll truly deserve.

Muriel Cannadine

REMORSE. A BORSTAL BOY'S CONTRITION

I can do nothing about what's in the past,
And today I am here in this place.
But I know I would give anything
Just to restore the smile to your face.

Dear mother I'm certain I've broken your heart,
I'm filled with remorse to have hurt you.
Why was I lead to step out of line?
To be shut in here? To desert you?

My whole being aches with desire to explain
That I'm feeling deeply your sorrow.
So I'm sure I really must work hard
To bring you a brighter tomorrow.

E Balmain

A WISH UPON MY ASS

War, famine
Death and disease
It's all so trivial
If you please

Petty, pathetic
Lies? I'm glad
To see something
You've never had

Global, national
Peace and prosper
I have escaped
What you foster

Truths, beliefs
Science and fiction
Can you escape
This tempting addiction?

Breaking, sharing
Bread and fish
Freedom from oppression
It is this I wish.

Alex Mcleod

A DAY OF HOPE

He sits so quiet, his face so pale,
When he moves he pulls on the rail.
When born he thrilled his dad and mum,
News was told he would not walk or run.
With patience and loving care
They did all they could for this one so fair.

Clever men cut with many a knife
To help this brave lad to have a better life.
With courage he will struggle and pray
That soon he will stand and move
His prayers answered, that will be his special day.

Glad Davies

I WISH

I wish to be around to see my babies grow
To love, teach and nurture them, protecting from all foe.

I wish to be around to see my children flower,
Into happy individuals, a proud mother every hour.

I wish to be around to see my grandchildren born.
To hold them and bond with them. A new generations dawn.

I wish to be around to see my mate grow old.
Reflecting on a happy life, memories of love and warmth, no cold.

Sharon Goodridge

MY WISH CAME TRUE

My wish came true
When I saw you
There in your wedding dress
A lovely bride I confess
With your flowers and your gown
And your veil floating down.
When you were small
Not very tall
You chased the lambs
As we roamed the hills.
Climbing the Cheviot
Out of breath
I made a wish
I cannot forget,
Today it came true
As I watched you wed
It made my day
With you in my arms
You called out with pleasure
And your usual charm
'Take a picture please,
Of me and my Gran.'

Maisie Bell

A CHILD'S WISH

Do not wish on a star wherever you are
For that will never come true
But put your faith in God's good grace
The faith that you must pursue
The little child knows someone is there
As she says her prayers each night
Dear God, please let me see again
Don't let it always be night.

Elizabeth Edwards

GOAL

To plan and score the winning goal
In a world cup final's match
And then be carried shoulder high
A hero on his patch

The crowd all cheering with delight
Becomes a deafening roar
As I acknowledge their applause
I couldn't wish for more

My passion for this game I find
Is one that will not die
The goal posts stand, for you to miss
However hard you try

I know I will succeed one day
It hasn't happened yet
But I with skill, will place that ball
At the very back of that net.

Mildred Jowett

I WISH

If I can, between that corner,
a corner between two worlds,
I wish to lay a bridge.
Hinges may rattle,
words may lose their voices
before they break the water

to bring forth life
on a bed of cold grey lines.
That will first cry and kick the ink
blind, carolling and sliding
perhaps upwards,
perhaps downwards
or outwards trimming the line.

I wish to plant roses
that are true blue, red and yellow.
Roses whose petals tumble the space
stained in the noise of a passing day,
petals that rosary around the heart.

Yes, I'll tattoo that line
if I can with all sorts of blossoms
whether alive or stillborn.
For I will breach that line
with a chain of words,
if I can. I'll make a wish.

Maroula Blades

I Wish I Was Slim

I wish
I was
Thin as
A pin.
I am
Sick of
Being told,
Of being
Scolded for
Being fat.
I am
That. I
Wish I
Was thin.

T Hartley

MY WISH

I wish I had the confidence
To do the things most people do
To feel at ease when someone says,
'Hello, how are you, how do you do?'
Instead I tremble, feel quite sick
Trying to put my thoughts in line
Thumping heart breath comes quick
Words don't seem to come on time
Everyday a challenge I try to overcome
Learn a little more each day
Walk instead of run.

Kathleen Morris

A SIMPLE WISH

I was never angry with you,
I was always angry with me,
Making my life so much harder
Than it really needed to be,
I was always jealous of you,
You seemed to have life all sorted out
Never worried knew what it was all about,
I see with clearer vision now,
Understand your sadness deep inside,
Put on a show for the boys
When you had no place left to hide,
It wasn't easy to feel
The one who was always left out,
Chose to close up my heart,
Held my tongue, but wanted to shout,
We weren't so very different, you and I,
We just dealt with pain in our own way,
Always brother and sister,
I wish we could be friends one day.

Zeta Hickey

WISHES GALORE

I wish my elder daughter happiness
I wish my younger daughter new hope in 2001
I wish good health to my son-in-law
I wish good fortune for those young ones in great need
I wish to see children being more polite to their parents
I wish fulfilment in the years to come when children today
          are parents
I wish that the younger generation will go back to organic food
I wish that our children will stop polluting the world
I wish the scientists of the future will not experiment on animals
I wish to hear the children of tomorrow say, the oceans are
          free from human rubbish
I wish to see the love of our young ones being appreciated
I wish that children's adorable chatter will give happiness to
          all who know them
I wish to hear children of today, now and forever do believe
          in God our father and Jesus Christ.

Alma Montgomery Frank

ONE CHILD'S SMILE

With one child's smile,
many hearts soar.

Grace, like a dove,
strength, lion's roar.

Up behind the sun,
back down through the clouds,
beaming light.

A wish for this day,
like magic, comes true,
smile, so bright.

Eva Byzio

MAKE A WISH WEEK

I put a coin in the wishing well
and then I heard a chime of a bell
a wishing star came shooting up
so I wished I had a pup.

When I found a 5p coin in my pocket
I wished it was a golden locket.
When I blew out my birthday candles
I wished my hair wouldn't get in a tangle!

Wishes are amazing things
you'll never guess the joy they bring.

Kelly Marie Tucker (8)

UNTITLED

I wish I had knowledge to succeed
To help my son be all he can be.

I wish I had a job helping others to see
Our Lord has forever set us free.

I wish for a holiday to help me relax,
To help me get back on the right tracks.

I wish for a home full of love
so I can share all of the above.

For my son and I, I wish for your strength
To follow the Lord through every length.

I wish forever to be
The best I can, living as me.

Anna Pullen

THE MAGIC BOX

I will put in my box
The deepest water of the Arctic ocean,
A courageous lifesaver in treacherous water,
A first smile of a baby.

I will put in my box
The silent minutes of a remembrance parade,
My bristling, bad tempered old cat,
My cute hamster,
A sunny day in Paris.

Alex Johnstone (7)

IMAGINATION

I am thinking of an island, I wish I could be there,
With the sun on my face and the cool sea breeze air,
Lying on the golden sand underneath a tree,
The only sound to hear is the gentle rolling sea.

The seagulls gliding high above in the deep blue sky,
Lying here, I wonder how it feels to fly,
In the far off distance is an outline of the shore,
I wish I had a boat so I could sail there and explore.

Out here it is so peaceful, there is not a soul in sight,
There's no man-made pollution to blacken out daylight,
The sea is clear as crystal and underneath lukewarm,
If you're looking hard enough you will see the fishes swarm.

In my imagination I can live without a care,
All I have to do is close my eyes and I am there,
This is my own island; God designed it just for me,
I cannot imagine any place where I would rather be.

Fern Anderson

THE LOVE SPELL

Because it's my last chance
I bought it, the love spell
(Bought in more ways than one.)

The man at 'Spooks' said it was a real one
Despite the plastic case and little ribbon
Tied in a bow, and mock-old parchment
With printed words in 'Olde English.'

He said it would work if you wanted it to
I believe him. I want it to.

I can't get through to you in real life
Not through the chatter of girls
And workaday problems, telephones ringing
And such. Not even when I stand up and shout
'Look at me, why don't you?'

So I've got this spell and late at night
When you're asleep, the words will rise
Like smoke in wispy fingers
And reach into your brain
And you'll be mine. Forever.

Not bad for eight pounds fifty.

Janet Saville

DRUMBEATS

Drumbeats in the velvet dark -
airborne spices, tonga bells -
soulful sitar, plaintive voice;
on veranda, lantern lit,
silver moths come out to dance.
I wish, I wish I could be there.

At jasmine-scented sundown
while the Imam called to prayer,
I once cycled down the Mall -
underneath the Banyan trees
with parrots squawking overhead -
Oh! How I wish I could be there.

To picnic by the Indus
on shish-kebabs and naans -
or watch the monsoon breaking
to turn the sand to mud -
water which ran away too soon -
I wish, I wish I could be there.

To see the lepers begging
and give what I could spare;
in thankfulness for being whole -
what poverty one sees!
Yet, when India's in your blood
you're glad that you are there.

I gave my heart to India -
though born in Western clime.
But Fate gives us a place to be -
a destiny to fulfil
and mine is here, but even so,
I wish, I wish I could be there!

Trixie Bee

WINTER

Under a leaden sky
Acres
Of snowfields devour
Suburban gardens.

A flock of starlings
Raucous
In their greed.

Blackbirds stark
Against
The carpet of snow.

A pair of blue tits
perform
Their acrobatics
On the
Spectral twigs of trees.

A wheatear plump
And
Restless in the morning.

While in the foreground
Dark with mystery
The footprints of an unknown
Animal.

Rupert Smith

DARTH RAMBO WISHES HE HAD A JOB

I'm Darth Rambo, unemployed and forty years old,
I've researched the International Space Station that's bold;
And created a written project describing about painting,
To paint the surface area of buildings writing
Using colours green, blue, white, yellow and red;
I could paint whole streets in this way,
But I've no equipment, savings, job or say.
Where can I paint this art once ripped,
I've created my first laid-out book manuscript;
I have poetry, short supernatural stories and illustrations,
Which is part of a volume for nations.
Now I am trying to publish the book,
To market it into a best selling look;
I'll accept an offer of a full-time job,
Of being an artist earning a writer's bob.
I'll even do both in the Leeds site,
And with preference, north or central Leeds lights;
I'll even work in Castleford, Bradford and Wakefield,
Doing hours of Monday to Friday which appealed.

Ian K A Ferguson

THE WAY I WISH

Ozone friendly
Pollution free
The way I wish
The world could be
Fresh clean rivers
Deep blue seas
Life infested meadows
Wise old trees
Elephant saved
And the whale swims free
The way I wish
The world could be

Alan Green

BALLOON RIDE REQUIRED

In hot air balloon I wish I could fly,
Sailing along, watching birds floating by.
I'd look at buildings, people and treetops,
I wouldn't want the short journey to stop.

Think I'd enjoy feeling of weightlessness,
As for the height reached I could not care less.
Upward, upward to the heavens we'd go,
Then drift with the contraption all aglow.

Unfortunately trips hard to obtain,
This unfulfilled wish for a ride remains.
But if I ever win the lottery,
I'd book a seat in the next basket for me.

S Mullinger

DOLPHINS

I wish I could swim with dolphins
In a warm and gentle sea,
I wish I could talk to dolphins
While they play alongside me.
I wish I could laugh with dolphins
With their cheeky, friendly faces,
I wish I could float with dolphins
To some wonderful sunlit places.
I wish I could learn from dolphins
As we play in sea and sun,
I wish I could hug a dolphin,
An extra-special one.

Katrina Shepherd

FOUR-LEAFED CLOVER

I will lie beside you
So you and I may lie
And count the stars that glow
And view the endless sky
And feel the cool green grass,
And hear the whispering wind
And watch the clouds that pass
And see if we can find
Ourselves a four-leafed clover.
And if you hold my hand
We need not search forever.
So come and lie with me
And when I feel you near
I know that I will see
My very precious four-leafed clover.

Joan E Blissett

TRAVELLING IN TIME

The Starship Enterprise glimmering out in space
Capturing the imagination of every child's gaze
Out there in a galaxy of shimmering lights
And watching are wee faces and eyes gripping tight
What wonders that are yet unknown
And that will yet transpire when we are grown
Then when we feel most vulnerable
And see a touch of something a little cruel
We cuddle our heads and hold our Teds
Till our cries are soothed and we are safe in bed

Yes, the stars tell us there is a time zone
And although sometimes we travel solitary, we are never quite alone
No one is there to touch or see
But the stars are watching over me
The guardian angels of the solar system
Their keen ears are always listening
Even someone groaning in a low tone
A star tinkles and becomes anxious that they are not alone
And now and again we leave a loved one behind
Yes for that we have to be strong
But maybe you know another angel is born

In life we are met by challenge for us to achieve
If we meet those endeavours then that angel in us believes
We then grow in honesty and truth
And the wider universe benefits from what is good
What was unknown when we were a child
Has transpired in life's long mile
And out there The Starship Enterprise
Hovers above with a smile in her eyes
Yes, she's really a big sister

On returning from my travels, a tear said I missed her
I thought I was hiding away
But secretly, I prayed for the day
When I would hear a click and the searchlight went electric
And from out of the sky, the voice simply said 'Hi!
This is Starship Enterprise.
Now that you're found all on board
    have tears of joy in their eyes.
        Welcome, welcome, we come in peace, because
        we've been overwhelmed by your good deeds.

    Reach out to the queen of the skies.
        Climb on board The Starship Enterprise.'

Anne R Cooper

MAKE A WISH

'Make a wish. Make a wish.' Was the little gnome's cry
As the girl at the Wishing Well said with a sigh.
'Oh, I so wish my playmates were here with me now
But the fact is they're poorly and I don't quite know how
I can assist them, try to help them, with problems so rare
I am helpless, almost useless and I do really care.
Can you guide me, perhaps advise me or at least tell me why
I make a wish?' - 'Make a wish.' Was the little gnome's cry.

As she gazed into the depths of the Well she could hear
Faint echoes of promises both far and from near.
'Are those fairies' she pondered, 'but why in a well?
I was always taught fairies lived down in the dell.'
'Make a wish. Make a wish.' Was the little gnome's cry.

But! Lest I forget it, I must tell you this,
Throw coins in the Wishing Well when you make your wish.
'And why is this so?' asked the girl in reply
'It's the price of a wish,' was the little gnome's cry.
'Make a wish. Make a wish. Make a wish.'

Dennis Macdonald Turberfield

PRECIOUS WISHES

Precious wishes
Like angel hair
Or fairy wings
Create rainbows of colour
Of 'what-might-be's'
In grey clouded minds
Warming sunshine
On gloomy days
These golden rays
Fill our souls
With hope
Anticipation
And countless joys
Happy thoughts
In routine lives
Building expectations
With intricate webs
Silken gossamer threads
Holding and catching
Our dreams and desires

Geraldine Laker

My Wish

Why do folk have to suffer
And always be in pain?
There is no respite from their anguish
Although they try in vain.

There must be someone, somewhere
Who has that special gift
Of using all his healing powers
To give those in pain a lift.

My wish is for that person
To introduce a balm
That would take away the suffering
Bring about a quiet calm.

We know their days are numbered,
But without the constant pain,
For a while their spirits would be raised
And they'd learn to smile again.

And finally they'd slip away
With their loved ones all around
Who will say a little prayer of thanks
That an answer has been found.

Norah Carter

MAKE A WISH

Make a wish for more tolerance
In our society today.
It needs great effort not just chance
Not just a game we choose to play.

Make a wish for equality
Not just in the calm countryside
But in each and every city
In fact, why not make it world wide?

Make a wish this day for freedom.
Freedom for body, soul and mind.
It should be for all, not just for some.
For people of each race and kind.

Make a wish for education.
It should help us to understand
The hopes of every nation
And people of every land.

Make a wish for more compassion
Towards each member of each race.
Ensure that it's not just a fashion.
In your heart please give it a place.

Make a wish that each one lives
To fulfil their own potential
In certain hope that each one gives
Something in return, substantial.

Make a wish now for world peace
From the four corners of the globe;
From Ireland to the Middle East
We must continue and to probe
Each day, each way our goal to find
No matter how much cost or grind.

Catherine Craft

FILTHY RICH

I wish I were a millionaire
For then I wouldn't have a care,
Wherever I could set my heart
It would be mine - a work of art,
A fancy car, everywhere I'd be a star.
To holiday in far-off shores,
Someone to do the nasty chores,
The best of food, and comfort too
No second-hand - all would be new.
But here I am and as I see
The pictures now on my TV.
I see a place where food is rare
The children hungry, sick and bare
A place of famine, war, disease
Where people beg on bended knees
Nowhere to really call a home
And life has left them all alone.
I realise as I see them
It's time for me to think again
For really, I don't have a care,
In fact, I am a millionaire.

John Hale

QUEST

I wish that in this life of mine
A cord which runs right through, I'd find
And make some sense of every season
To give events their place and reason.

If I could find the hidden key
And use what my parents invested in me
That through circumstance and many a rain
Might somehow become another's gain

If I could offer what hands can't hold -
A prize that is neither bought nor sold
Then I might rest in knowing my place
Which now I see dimly, but then face to face.

But surely that cord has been there, unbroken
Like a vow that remains from the moment it's spoken
And I believe I will know with the fullness of time
That cord which ran through this life of mine.

Avril Hale

CONTENTMENT

I wish for clouds of cotton fields,
That float gently over lakes and hills.
I wish for a breeze that gently blows,
Tranquillity from the stream that flows.
I wish for a world where no one fights,
A place filled with love and equal rights.

I wish for hills that full of heather,
Where goats and cattle tether.
I wish for pastures that are ever green,
Where everyone is a king or queen.
I wish for contentment as otters play,
A place where men their fears allay.

I wish for birds to sing all day long,
So that I may accompany them in song.
I wish I had wings so that I could fly,
That first break of dawn to never die.
I wish for peace where disaster ends,
For all mankind to make amends.

Sandra Dahl

THE SHOOTING STAR

There are many ways to make a wish
I have tried quite a few
And even though I was patient
None of them came true

This was in my black period
Before I met my wife
When things kept going wrong
Each year of my life

I was smoking yet another cigarette
Leaning against my car
When something moved across the sky
It was a shooting star

I made a wish upon that star
What had I got to lose
Maybe someone would come along
Disperse those sad old blues

A friend I had known for a year
Phoned to invite me out
She had been trying to find the words
To tell me how she felt

Now married for twenty-three years
It seems like yesterday
And we have three lovely children
Who were a bonus along the way

I still remember that magic night
I know I always will
When I wished upon a shooting star
And my dreams all came true

Trevor J Skitt

A MOTHER'S PRAYER

Rest quietly now my little one.
Close your eyes for the day is done.
I will whisper a tale of Sir Knight so bold,
A beautiful princess and a pot of gold.
Fierce dragon defeated, a brave man was he;
The villagers rejoiced as they were set free.

Sleep softly now my darling one.
The moon and stars have replaced the sun.
Let your mind drift to a land that is new,
A time and a place where wishes come true.
Every child has a home with people who care.
Animals are protected and breathe clean, fresh air.

Dream of happy times my sweet one.
In lush green meadows, dance and run.
Smell the scents of nature as you pass by.
Let the wind lift your arms as in the air you fly,
Over treetops and houses observing the ground,
See children celebrating the unity they've found.

Wake with a smile my beloved one.
An exciting day awaits, endless hours of fun.
Remember precious thoughts as you drifted to sleep,
Let no one steal them, they are yours to keep.
Live in a fairytale castle, embrace sparkling sunbeams,
Believe in yourself, all of your wishes and dreams.

Karen Davies

A DARK WORLD

Discreetly observed
this young child and mother
seated before me.

Strangely disturbing
his hesitant eager speech
vulnerable mouth
pallid perfection of skin

Her tender watchfulness.

When, after the journey,
she took his arm firmly
to guide him safely,
his wide-eyed gratitude
revealed to me harshly

His dark world of blindness.

Much moved, moving away,
I heard the child say
. . . Whose was that hand
which touched my cheek?

I wish that I could see

Louise Rogers

WISHING

I wish I lived in a castle
with servants to wait on me
And not have to look in the larder -
and wonder what's for tea!

Diamonds and bracelets and
beautiful things,
Money galore and glistening rings.
Though I must confess
it's much the best,
To wish for good health
and happiness.

E Petty

MAKE A WISH, MAKE A MARRIAGE, MAKE A CHILD . . .

Before I meet my Maker,
I'd like to make a wish,
My honey's one heartbreaker!
She really is a dish!
She fills my heart with yearning,
No use denying now!
Indeed, my heart is burning!
I love that girl, and how!
My wish is thus quite basic . . .
Because my love is true . . .
She's the one that I would pick
And be devoted to . . .
My wish is that she loved me,
Enough for wedding bells!
Never to have rebuffed me,
For there is no-one else . . .
I miss her in the morning!
I miss her all day long!
And with each new day dawning,
My hopes return so strong!
Is it too much to mention?
Beyond what God can do?
Does God like my intention,
Enough to see it through?
No heirs have I to honour
This love I truly bear . . .
No babe that clings upon her
In search for milk to share . . .
What use is life without love?
What purpose does it serve?
Is my 'marriage wish' enough?
God grant us Heaven on Earth!

D K F Martindale

A WISH

A wish of yours has come to nought
Some dream has not come true
The hopes are cherished one by one
Alas they've died on you
Yet in your heart if one small flame
Still flickers - then you may
Somehow, sometime, dream other dreams
That will come true some day.

Ann Grimwood

I'VE MADE A WISH!

I wish I was young and in my prime,
Not just watching the sands of time.
I wish I could have helped folks more
Been more willing than I was before.
I wish that I had gone to college
That I had been fulfilled with knowledge.
I wish I had been endowed with wings,
So that I could soar above the mundane things.
I wish I had the arts and graces,
To fit in all those 'special places'.
I wish that I had worn a smile
To make every day, just seem worthwhile.
I wish I could have waved my wand,
To make pain and suffering soon abscond.
I wish I hadn't watched so much 'tele'.
Spent more time reading Keats and Shelley.
I wish politicians kept their word,
And that words of wisdom could be heard.
I wish for all the joys of love
I'll kneel and pray to God above.
Some wishes He will make come true,
And He'll do His very best for you.
The very best is all you can ask,
And the ability to do the hardest task!

Edith Antrobus

A WISH FROM THE HEART

My friend Joanna looked very glum,
So I asked if to tea she'd come.
As she sat and ate her cake
She told me what caused her heart to ache:
'It's Maggie Daly. She's horrid to me.
She's a bully. Can't you see?
I just wish she'd go away
Leave me alone for just one day.'

For a while I sat and thought,
Then down the garden, the fairies I sought.
Down behind the oak I found them,
And carefully explained the problem.

The fairy queen said 'You're right to ask
For our help to complete this task.
Bullying is something we hate to see,
So I'll grant you a wish to set Joanne free!'

I took the bottled wish away,
And wondered just what words to say.
Then that night as I lay in bed
The right wish-words came into my head:
'My friend Joanne, is very sad.
Anyone who bullies is very bad.
Whether you're at work or school -
Give up bullying, or you're a fool!
You cause hurt to people every day
With your nasty bullying ways.
There's just one thing that I wish for,
For all bullies to *stop!* And bully no more.'

Brenda Jane Williams

WHICH WISH WILL COME TRUE?

Which wish will come true when she grows up?
Will she be a dancer?
Will she work at all her steps
Till a producer will chance her?

Which wish will come true when she grows up?
Will she go upon the stage?
Will she practise day and night
To merit a decent wage?

Which wish will come true when she grows up?
An air hostess trim and smart?
Will she diet and keep herself slim
In order to get the part?

Which wish will come true when she grows up?
A children's nanny maybe?
Seeing her charges are well behaved
Yet keeping them all very happy!

Which wish will come true when she grows up?
Be a nurse or even a doctor?
Will she study the science of healing
For years, and then even more?

There are so many things to do in this life,
But whatever you choose, remember this.
You *must* enjoy doing it, you *must* strive hard at it,
Your heart *must* be in it, and your days will be bliss!

Christopher Head

OUR GRANDCHILDREN

My wish for them

For a world of peace
Without the horrors of war
A safe and happy childhood
Cocooned within a home of love
May they learn
Sharing and caring
Right from wrong
Politeness and manners
Patience and kindness
Compassion and love
As they journey through this life
With knocks, setbacks and strife
Learn to take each in their stride
Holding their heads high with pride

The innocence I now see
Wide-eyed, looking at me
Standing there eager to learn
Incessant questions at every turn

These bright enquiring minds
Be nurtured as they grow
And may all their aspirations
Plans and dreams come true
In *everything* they do.

Sheila A Waterhouse

I WISH I HAD WINGS

I wish I had wings, and was able to fly,
What a wonderful thing that would be,
To be able to soar right up into the sky,
Where no one on earth could see me.

No need any longer to wait in a queue,
Wherever I wished I could go.
And whenever I found I had nothing to do
I could zoom off and no one would know.

If the weather was cold, and it made me feel blue
I could flutter away to the sun.
I would soak up the warmth, and be happy right through
And soon I'd be ready for fun.

I shall never grow wings, so my wish can't come true
But still, it's been fun just to dream.
And today in my glider, I'll climb into the blue
That's as near as I'll get, so it seems.

Jean Gray

ESPECIALLY FOR YOU

Children you are so special
You reach so many hearts
Though your plights are life-threatening
You still seem to merry-along
You give so much
And ask for so little in return
All you ask for
Are your basic needs
Food, water, shelter, warmth
These few, would just be enough for you
Yet day after day your lives are fading away
That's why for you today
I'll take a moment to write these few words.
My new found meditation line
I'll use to make a wish for you.

Oh glorious future I know you are thine
Bless these Third World children
That they may be hungry no more.

Carolie Pemberton

MAKE A WISH - COWBOY

If I could have a wish come true
A cowboy I would be
And ride the range on my trusty steed
A piebald named Midnight Blue

I'd gallop off with my Stetson and chaps
And lasso the steers amidst all the cheers
Forgetting my fears, then perhaps
We'd stop for a drink, because after all
It's very thirsty work

It's hot and it's dusty
And sometimes quite blustery
But I love it, it's really stimulating
A fire we'd light, later that night
And quietly sit there debating

A guitar would be strumming
Whilst we were all humming
Sitting around the camp-fire
Our baked beans we'd eat, with potatoes and meat
Then to bed, before we all tire.

We'd awaken refreshed, after our rest
To start back for home - what a day!
For we'd headed 'em up, and rounded 'em in
Back to the OK Coral - okay.

If I could have a favourite wish
That's what my wish would be.

Phyllis Lorraine Stark

I WISH

I wish for people to forget,
The laws of gravity.
I wish for people to forget,
Why we have to eat.
I wish for people to forget,
That the world is round.
I wish for people to forget,
What it is to live - and die.
I wish for people to forget,
That fate doesn't rule.
I wish for people to forget,
How to walk.
I wish for people to forget,
That Earth is not alone in the galaxy.
I wish to have the world in ignorance,
I wish for these things to be left for *me* to discover,
I wish
For adventure!

Hollie Lewis (12)

THE JOURNEY

I wish I could take your forthcoming burdens child
And to ease from you the load
So the passage of life you will travel
Will be a walk down a beautiful road

A road where you will never learn
What it feels like to suffer pain
Or heartaches that will bring you to your knees
As you seek your life's goals to attain

For love is the one thing of which we never get sated
For always we try to give or earn more
For wealth, fame, possessions, soon lose their appeal
So my child love is what you should search for

I wish I could take your forthcoming burdens child
Before the first step on that journey you tread
For I have learned how our own foolish desires
Dictate how our false hungers are fed.

Don Woods

A DREAM COME TRUE

If I had a magic wand
I'll tell you what I'd do,
I'd make a wish, then wave the wand,
And hope it would come true.

For my wish would be, for the rest of my life,
I would enjoy good health.
Cos money can't buy you this,
Even tho' you have great wealth.

Then I'd ask if I could share my wish,
With the rest of my family too.
Because a lifetime of perfect health,
Would be a dream come true.

Jean Hendrie

TROUBLED MIND

What a great idea at the time
I hadn't the heart to decline
Creative writing, prose and rhyme
for lonely anxious, troubled of mind

Nervous, fraught - how would they retort
with this stranger and her writing course
The drop-in centre welcomed me in
bright decor, warmth and gossipy din

Pool table, computer, music, TV
A haven from pressure is what I see
For the broken in spirit, bent in grief
To lick their wounds, find their feet

Suspicious, doubtful, often worse
Toward this stranger with a course
I chat away for best part of the day
they soon relax and seem unfazed

I weather several difficult months
Very often they've taken the hump
Their highs, lows, fights with the foe
The mental demons that refuse to go

The joy when they're all feeling great
They jokingly chide me when I'm late
Raring to go, now seems a good time
For writing, reading and some rhyme!

Astrid Hymers

MY FAVOURITE PRESENT

A doll -
  With ebony hair
  And deep brown eyes
  Was what I wished for
  When I was just four.

My parents -
  They said 'Too expensive,
  We can't afford that.'
  And because they'd said no
  My Christmas would simply come . . . and go.

Me -
  I was the little girl
  With the hugest grin
  When my wish came true . . .
  My parents were strangely happy too.

  (I don't know why,
  Santa only gave them slippers!) . . .

Debby Aistrup-Brown

ALL MEN - EVERYWHERE

I wish that all men - everywhere
Should seek the Lord today
As I look around I see
Chaos and decay

Will we leave our children
A God-forsaken place?
No! It's time for all men - everywhere
To turn and seek his face

Listen all men - everywhere
Stop and take a look
Then see what God has written
Within that good old book

The maker of men - everywhere
Left us the manual of life
Within it lies the answers
To all man's woes and strife

Would that all men - everywhere
Happ'ly seek the Lord today
That all the troubles of mankind
Might prayer-fully melt away.

Norah Page

I LONG TO SEE . . .

I long to see . . .
> the world set free and living peacefully,
> with no more hatred, envy, greed, or even bigotry.

I long to see . . .
> bowed low in chains, the 'father of all lies',
> with no escape, no more chances, standing
> with downcast eyes.

I long to see . . .
> him suffering, as he's made others suffer over time,
> his deceived servants I pity, but I hate this enemy
> of mine!

I long to see . . .
> him on his knees, before my Lord and King,
> answering for all the misery he did bring.

I long to see . . .
> him locked away, deep within the pit,
> with Jesus, the Rock, sealed across - a perfect fit!

I long to see . . .
> an end to sickness, pain and strife,
> with billions of souls enjoying bountiful, eternal life.

I long to see . . .
> along with them, my dear, dear Saviour's face,
> to daily walk and talk with Him and live
> within His grace.

I long to see . . .
> my Father God, who created such variety,
> in every facet of nature and in every face I see.

I long to see . . .
> my Comforter, my Guide and Counsellor, the
> Holy Spirit, whose teaching has helped my spirit soar.

I long to see . . .

> Them all together, the Holy Trinity,
> living with all the ransomed souls, eternally set free.

Amen

Margi Hughes

KIRSTY

I wish we could make Kirsty better,
Let her dance and sing just like before,
And stop the cancer taking her, from our sunny shore,

I wish we could turn the clock back,
To those happy days on memory etched and lain,
I'm desperate to do something to take away her pain,

I wish we were brave,
Like Kirsty has become,
She is our inspiration, our life, our sun,

I wish I knew an angel
Who could save her from her fate,
Angel please come quickly, before it is too late,

I wish with all my heart,
That I could take her place,
For I have lived my life, and she's had but a trace,

I wish there was something we could do,
But we are helpless, standing in her wings,
Hopes and prayers are all we can bring,

I remember her life,
Full of laughter, full of fun,
Everybody loved Kirsty, she is a special one,

I remember her smile,
It was a beacon on the hill,
Her smile lives within me still,

I pray for a miracle,
Because time is running short,
Only a miracle can this tragedy abort,

Then one bright and sunny morning,
I just knew this was the day,
When Kirsty on silver wings quietly slipped away.

P J Littlefield

A WISH FOR A WORLD OF SMILES

Touch somebody's life with a smile
Touch somebody's life for a while
You can make a difference to the lonely or the sad
To a man or a woman, a girl or a lad
Touch somebody's life with a word
Someone may be longing to be heard
Touch somebody's life with a deed
Something only small can fill a need

Touch somebody's life and you find
You will gain great peace of mind
Spread a little warmth, spread a little care
Spread a little laughter if you dare
Share a joke, share a tear,
Sometimes it's good just to be near
Give a little love, open up your heart
To make a better world, let's play a little part

You can make a difference with just a minute of your day
The difference will reflect and joy will come your way
So touch somebody's life with a smile
And you can make each day worthwhile.

Maureen Condron

I WISH

I wish I could recapture moments in life
And forget all the sorrows and the strife.
Events of happiness, and all the pleasure
Collected thoughts to savour, and treasure

Childhood days of innocence, and youth
Sixpence from a fairy, for first lost tooth
Nursery and school, learning A, B, C's
A kiss off mother, when scraping my knees

Teenage years, at the local dance
Weighing up the talent for a bit of romance
Going to the pub, for a first beer
Football matches at which to shout and cheer

Meeting my intended, and our first kiss
Settling down to a life of marital bliss
The birth of our children, one, two, three
Guiding them through their lives, trouble free

Through all the years that have flown
And now with five grandchildren of our own
I can look back at past times gone amiss
Thank the Lord God, and say, I wish

Thomas William Evans

MAKE A WISH

If I could make a wish come true
I'd look to my God to see me through
Any way I walk in life
To be free from illness worry or strife.

To watch my children and yours too
Grow up with care, hearts for me and you
To give a kind word in their daily life
To anyone they made contact with show their light.

Their lamp of light showing in eyes
Young people, old people the truly wise
A helping hand for whoever they meet
At work, at home or in the street.

To pass on to others their skills and knowledge
To create a world of love and encourage
Encourage others to never give in
To stay on track and to win.

Enter the race with love in their hearts
Even when troubles start
Obstacles passed, the road is clear
Care for each other, stay sincere.

I'd wish for caring communities
The place where we live, you and me
Safer, healthier places to live
Where love reigns if we only give.

Flossie

I WISH

I'm 80 plus now and I wish I was younger
I'd like lots more time before I go under,
I wish I was slim, I've been plump for so long
Can I sell off my 'flab'? It could go for a song!
I wish I was taller. I was once called Swan-neck
But where's that neck now? It's just gone. Oh heck!
I wish crime would lessen, instead it gets worse
Out flicks a knife, someone else in a hearse.
I wish people were kinder, they used to be so.
Or do I see the past through a rosy glow?
I wish and I wish that all wishes came true
But maybe, one day, they will for you.

M A Griffin

PEACE OF MIND

I wish, I long for days set free,
from the baggage of life,
a growing burden to me . . .
Tho' I live for each day . . .
I need to act:
to pare down belongings.
This is a fact.
I used to think that the
main cause -
was to spare loved ones
these burdensome chores
But first and foremost
now I know
I need clutter-free living
Before home I go!

Patricia Lawrence

I WISH

I wish I was a Grandma, with young ones on my knee,
I could tell them little stories of how my life used to be.
I could rock them in the cradle and read them nursery rhymes
I'd give them so much love, we would have such happy times.
I could take them to the seaside, or even to the zoo,
Give them little treats like Grandmas seem to do.
But I'm not destined to be a Grandma, for fate has played its part.
But my cherished memories of motherhood are stored safely
                                                      in my heart.

Margaret Meadows

WISHES THAT WHISPER

To welcome each and every dawn
Enhanced by birds in song
And *hear* good news once in a while
Where things are right not wrong

To *see* a rainbow far beyond
Raindrops glistening in the sun
Like pearls upon the petals
A joy for everyone

To *walk* beneath the moonlight
And enjoy the starlit sky
Day-dreaming in the pastures
And feel that I could fly

To *feel* the touch of caring
A hand, a hug, a kiss
Considering needs of others
Should never go amiss

To *talk* with great sincerity
My love of words to share
Bringing inner happiness
To all who seem to care

I would say my deepest wishes
Are things you cannot buy
Nature's gifts so precious
And they do not tell a lie.

Gillian M Ward

IMPATIENCE

When I was young and Christmas was near
I used to think it'll *never* be here -
I crossed off the days - glad to be rid,
I never once thought I'd be sorry I did!
When I turned 16 I thought *yes* at last
- but then oh how quickly that feeling went past.
I longed for eighteen, and then twenty-one
never once thinking how much of life's gone.
I longed to be married with kids of my own
- well now I've got them and look how they've grown.
In no time at all, my babies were men
- and that's when I wished I could do it again.
I realise now that it's easy to say
I wish I had not wished so much time away!

Carol Jackson

JUNE IN THE SOUTH

Sitting on my old garden seat one day
I just wished I could stop the clock,
The month of June would be ideal I thought
Colour is running wild in the gardens,
Borders looking so pretty and fresh.

Birds tweeting away,
Insects humming on the wing,
Hedgehogs fully awake now,
Lawn mowers chugging along.

Such a lot to do quite suddenly
So please stop the clock.
Let me savour the lovely colours,
The perfume of the roses, honeysuckle and pinks.
That warmth of the summer sun.
Winter will come along quite soon enough I feel sure.

Valerie Willan

MY PET WISH

I love all animals big and small
I don't care if they're ten feet tall.
I'd love a Kitten, I'd love a Frog
But best of all, I'd like a Dog.
I'd like a Labrador, golden or black
I'd like a Collie, I'd give him a snack.
My wish would be to have either one
We'd chase each other and have some fun!

Sarah Boon (8)

I WISH

I wish I could grow back my hair
It's gone and it just isn't fair
I wish I was shorter
I wish I'd not grown through my hair.

I wish I had long flowing locks
Like some ladies who have pretty frocks,
I wish I had a mane so supreme
And I wish I did not have to dream.

I wish I had back my fine waves
And I fear the tide has gone out.
I wish I could regain my youth
And count every hair that drops out.

I wish I could grow back moss
With a mane just like my boss,
For she is a bird, so I have heard,
I wish I could grow back my hair.

Derek J Morgan

MY WISH

I wish I were a Royal Ballet dancer
Graceful and petite
Dancing there without a care
My heart and soul complete

I worked so hard to get this far
My heart and soul put in
Rest for a while that I shall
Then hard work shall begin

When I'm alone and feeling sad
I begin to dance
Then I feel glad, I have such a gift
To even have the chance

But behind my smile awaits a small child
Scared and incomplete
Thinking what would happen
If her dream she did not meet

So there I sit and think of it
This wish I want so much
If only I could fulfil my dream
Or just to have one touch

So now I hope that you believe
Whatever your dream takes
If you believe, you can succeed
Then your dream awaits

Heather White (14)

MY DREAM HOME

This quaint cottage with lattice windows
Fancy barge boards and gates of rail
A notice board pushed in the hedge
To advertise this place is for sale

The porch was covered in roses
And the roof scallop-edge in gold thatch
They showed me the lawn and flower beds
A garden of herbs by the vegetable patch

White beehives under the apple trees
With a rustic seat in a grassy nook
A sloping path by a rock cascade
Leading to a clear rippling brook

Beyond the fence are fields of sheep
I stood there taking in the view
In the fresh air, peace and quiet
This could be my wish come true

The old cottage is cosy and warm
With a brick fireplace and old beams
On the kitchen range a kettle sings
This must be the place of my dreams

Now I have met the local people
Looking around the village was just fine
Family and grandchildren liked my wish
So wishing this cottage will be mine

Rose Rawlings

BORN TO EXPLORE

Wish,
Could be a shock;
But find comfort,
Touching my simple heart.

To wake,
When the soul;
Desires, it be so.

To wander the curiosities,
Persuasion,
In life's spirit.
Those little,
Complex,
Bold, soft;
The soul encounters,
As days stream.

To venture, and chance on a spot,
Well appointed;
Cross-legged, waiting for sunrise.

The soft fingertips,
Of the early sun;
Touching soul.

Small, infinitely exquisite wings,
Born to explore, the magnificence,
Within everyday peace;
Those secret treasures,
Awaiting discovery,
And celebration.

Wish to wander free,
And reap,
Of precious song.

Rowland Warambwa

I Wish I Had A Different Car

I wonder what it might be like
A new Rolls Royce or Jag,
Better than a two-mile hike
To ring someone to bring the breakdown van.

Yes, my car breaks down and doesn't make a sound,
Oh, when will that nice AA man come?
I wouldn't need him if I had a new Mondeo,
That would take me from A to B.

It's raining now, still no help is near,
Gosh, how I wish I had a beer.
What's this, the nice AA man is here,
What's wrong with my car will soon be clear.

He bangs down the bonnet and dusts his hands,
A job well done, now I'll get on home.
I know my motor wouldn't let me down,
Home's not far, still I wish I had a different car.

Jean Foster

THE PLEASURES OF THE SEA

I wish you could see the dolphins performing by the boat.
I'd choose the day when it was fine and then you'd be afloat.
They really are gregarious, spinning in mid-air, surfing on the waves,
Bow-wave riders appearing from nowhere.

I wish you could see the dolphins when the sea is blue.
You'd catch a glimpse of silver as they flashed in front of you;
They know how to avoid their foes by hiding in the deep,
Then re-emerge above the waves as if they'd been asleep.

I wish that you could see the dolphins - it's such a happy sight.
You'd love to feel the sunshine and smell the herbs at night.
Alas, I know that time is short - there is no turning back -
But we must preserve our memories and keep things right on track.

I wish you could see the dolphins as each year they return,
Surfing across the water, taking it in turns,
It really is very pleasing - something to preserve.
One never knows the moment when tragedy occurs
To spoil the joys of nature that everyone enjoys.

Barbara Stannard

NKOSI

Nkosi, what a name.
This wish is for you, little boy,
That when you live with the angels
The world will remember your words
And change, change, change.

Tolerance, friendship and understanding
Was the plea you made.
We are all human and need love, you said.
Let your words be heard
And may the world always remember you . . .
And change, change, change.

Jeanette Walker

MY FAVOURITE WISH

I wish there was no cruelty
to animals on land
I wish that instead of killing
man would give a helping hand.

Foxes hunted for pleasure
I wish they were left to live
to amble at their leisure
in their homeland we were meant to give.

I wish dolphins and whales
were left to swim alone
without the constant worry
of a net or harpooning zone.

I wish dogs and cats
were not treated bad
thrown out and abandoned
from the only home they had.

I wish that little lambs
were not slaughtered for a meal
and that man would realise
that animals can feel.

Animals have a right to be here
and to be treated in a respectful way
This is my wish
that I wish would start today.

Lisa Kelly

THE ARK THAT NOAH BUILT

There were kangaroos, how do you do
A grizzly bear, two made a pair
A horny rhino who spoilt the lino
A lazy lion, the clothes he'd try on
A cunning fox who wore red socks
A tall giraffe who couldn't laugh
Who lived inside the ark that Noah built

There was a pike who rode a bike
A silvery cod, near to God
A pair of whales who weathered gales
A slender shark who loved the dark
A mighty trout who swam about
A wiggly eel who always kneeled
Who swam beside the ark that Noah built

There was a swallow, hard to follow
A bumblebee, flying free
A humming bird who loved the word
A pelican who got a tan
A dragonfly, a handsome guy
A humble wren who avoided men
Who flew above the ark that Noah built

John Mark

I REALLY WISH

I wish, I wish, I really wish
That trees weren't quite so tall,
That lofty branches often seem
Ready to break or fall.
That leaves would not drop quite so soon,
Leaving the branches bare,
But could stay a little longer,
To keep the raindrops from my hair.

I wish that each day sunshine shone
Directly on my roses,
Bringing them all to bud and bloom
And tantalise our noses.
Their scent so sweet and cultured,
More than any other flowers,
Could banish all my cares and doubts
And drive away life's showers.

The snowdrop greets the early spring
With a whiteness oh so pure;
It speaks of charity and love
In its tender, frail allure.
I wish that, in my daily life,
I might display more clearly,
What nature in her floral garb
Has symbolised more nearly.

I wish, dear Father, to enjoy
Your gifts and grace so free,
For I know that for this very cause
My Saviour died for me.
So move me, Lord, at this late hour,
To give to the One in Three,
All glory, might and majesty,
From genuflected knee.

Keith Allison

MAGIC MOMENTS

Close your eyes and make a wish,
And try hard not to cry,
Send your wish up to the stars,
So high up in the sky,
A twinkling star is magic,
It can make your dreams come true,
So close your eyes and make a wish,
Teddy will come home to you.

Walking through the wooded park,
On such a lovely day,
Teddy saw his family,
So he decided he would stay,
Just to play and have some fun,
And picnic in the park,
I am sure he will come home,
With Daddy now it's dark.

So dry your eyes my little love,
Your wish it will come true,
I know the magic starlight
Will bring teddy back to you,
You can hug and kiss him,
And show him how much you care,
And you will know your teddy bear,
Will always be there.

Lesley Allen

TRUE FRIENDS

I've been labelled with a syndrome
I'm not very pretty
I move around quite awkwardly
But I don't want your pity
I want you just to see me
Not my illness or disease
That I have inner beauty
Will you look deeper please?

I want to have true friends
Who won't look at me as weird
I know that I am different
How the people they have stared
Others don't want to know
So they avoid my path
My pain is more than physical
I'd tell you if you'd ask.

I've met some kind people
Though few and far between
Who treat me as an equal
A significant human being
How I long to meet much more
Not just for my own sake
But for other children like me
To find the icing on the cake.

Will you be one of these
Who will take or make the time
To reach out in genuine care
And become a friend of mine?

Carol Small

I WISH, I WISH

If I could wish for anything, it wouldn't be for wealth.
It wouldn't be for a fancy car, nor even my own health.

I'd ask for some more time, to spend with my dear mum
Who was sadly taken from me, and I didn't miss her till she'd gone.

When someone's always there for you, you don't realise their worth.
It doesn't really hit you, till they're no longer on this earth.

She'd have made a lovely grandmother, but that was sadly not to be.
The kids will have to make the most of what they have in me.

But I'll model myself on her, and be what she wanted me to be.
And I'll have the bond with my sweet kids, like the bond she had
with me.

So If I could have just one wish, if only for a day.
I'd spend it with my dear mum, and this is what I'd say.

Mum there's not a day goes by
When I don't think of you,
Wishing we could do the things
That mums and daughters do.

So wherever I may be
And whatever I may do,
There will always be a special space
In my heart for you.

Lots of love
always
xxx

Lynn Brown

AS IF WISHING WASN'T

I wish I could
    Tell ears of barely
        With this voice of August
            In indescribable light
            The brilliance and magnitude of Christ.

What wishing, accomplished,
    In summer's language
        What it is to break the earth
                Irreversibly

Through an old radio
    Become the proof of dreams
        The only proof needed
        Of a miracle,

Felt in a disembodied guitar's
    Evangelical heart.

Wish I were Venus between starless cities
    And not this tiny constellation
        In the skies perfect, deep blue apparatus,

Wish I were audible,
    To every breathing mortal,
        For one celestial song.

As true as beautiful
    As immaterial.
        Could explain to this world,
            As cynical as inexhaustible,
That I saw your wish come,
        Through melancholy
            True.

K Adamson

My Wish

I wish I was taller so I could see
Above the heads in front of me.
I wish my legs would grow some more
So I could walk more than before.
To be tall and brave and strong
This wish surely cannot be wrong.
To look at people in the eye
As they slowly pass me by.
If only I could taller be
I would truly be a different me.
All eager, looking forward to
So many different jobs to do.
For being taller I would see
Above the heads in front of me.

Betty Harper

I Wish

I wish I was a famous artist.
Lived my life to the full,
Wish I could produce a masterpiece
Like Gainsborough or Constable.
I'd travel to London or Paris maybe,
Mix with people of high class and nobility,
With splashes of colour, I'd paint with true feeling.
On small, or large canvas reaching high as the ceiling.
I'd have ladies and gentlemen sitting for me
All dressed up in their grand finery.
But the countryside would call, and that's where I'd rather be
And I'd dream my exhibit would hang by
The greats in the Tate Gallery.

Hazell Dennison

I WISH

I wish we all were young again
And young would always stay
Minutes hours months and years
Grow old and pass away

I wish we couldn't see again
The things we shouldn't see
Touch taste hear or smell
The things that shouldn't be

I wish it all could be again
The way it used to be
One root
One branch
One tree

I wish we all were young again
And young would always stay
Restless days and adult ways
Grow old and pass away

Oliver Eadie

I WISH . . .

People using hands to heal and help
Words of praise spoken every day
Smiles on faces, joy in hearts
I wish . . .
The world's family sharing
and caring
Hope for the future,
peace in the world
Love and friendship
Happiness for all
I wish . . .

Elisha Hardman (8)

I WISH...

People's smiles to last forever
Laughter to echo around the world
Kindness to touch people's hearts
I wish . . .
The dove of peace to
Spread wings of love
Happiness and harmony for all
Everyone to be friendly
And forgiving
I wish . . .

Sam Brown (7)

WHAT IS YOUR WISH?

I wish to go to Disneyland -
                    lots of fun!
I wish my nana could be young again -
                    we could play together!
I wish the school never had holidays -
                    I could learn more!
I wish the country could be cleaner -
                    nice and tidy!
I wish the world could be filled with nice people -
                    no more wars!
I wish the planet could be peaceful -
                    stop wars now!

Paul Blowers (8)

WISH LIST

Wise inventive space hopes
Watching incredible super heroes
World is supplying hungry
Wonderful imaginative surprise holiday
Wandering in starry happiness
Winter icicles store health.

Jordan Tyrrell (8)

WHAT IS YOUR WISH?

I wish I had beautiful golden hair and fairy wings
So I could fly with the doves.
I wish my family had lots of money
We could be rich and do anything we wanted.
I wish my school was in Disneyland
Just imagine Mickey Mouse as head teacher!
I wish the country had peace and harmony
No fighting or hurting just fun and laughter.
I wish the world could be less violent
Angry volcanoes and earthquakes to be calm and still.
I wish the planet could be a nicer place to live
No nasty pollution slowly destroying it!

Tina Scott (8)

WISH LIST

World in safe hands.
Winning incredibly sunny holidays.
World invents supreme happiness.
Wonderful ingredients save helpless.
World inspector says 'hope'.
Witnessing impressive starry heavens.

Kirsty Bunney (8)

I WISH . . .

The whole world to sing in harmony.
Colourful rainbows to brighten our days.
Special moments to give everyone a happy glow.
I wish . . .
Warmth and love filling hearts and mind.
Happiness and peace to rule our lives.
Laughter ringing throughout the world.
I wish . . .

Peter Caveney (8)

WHAT IS YOUR WISH?

I wish I had beautiful shiny wings
to fly in the sky
I wish my family was kind and helpful
I wish my school was an exciting adventure park
I wish the country had lots of harmony
I wish the world was full of peace
I wish the planet was a friendly place to live.

Jessica Boden (7)

WHAT IS YOUR WISH

I wish for a sister because I get lonely.
I wish my family wouldn't grow old because I love them.
I wish my school had no problems or worries
Because we should all be . . .
I wish my country had no aggressive people
Because others copy them.
I wish the world had no floods because
People have to start all over again.
I wish the planet could live in peace and harmony!

Ashleigh O'Wellen (8)

WISH LIST

Whistling in sweet harmony
Wearing interesting sparkly hats
Watching impressive super heroes
Welcome in solar houses
We investigate space hospital
War is stopped here.

Rebecca Young (8)

WISH LIST

Winning invisible super heroes
Winning incredible sunny holidays
Walking into secret hideaways
Writing in super hieroglyphics
Weather is sunny here
Wonderful inventions spreading happiness.

Peter Halliday (7)

WHAT IS YOUR WISH?

I wish for a tortoise and a cat
We could have such fun together
I wish for my family to love one another.
Everyone smiling and giving hugs.
I wish for my school to be filled with kind
Happy voices on the playground, helping each other
I wish for the country to be warm and friendly
A comfortable place to live with people who care
I wish for the world to be peaceful
Health and happiness for all
I wish for the planet to breathe fresh air
Free from rubbish and pollution.

Thomas Mohan & Bethany Pennington (8)

WISH

I wish for peace,
I wish for food,
I wish for you,
I wish for myself,
I wish for good times,
Most of all I wish for a wish for a friend.

Samuel Gallagher

WISHING

I wish for snowy white horses
With long flowing manes;
Floating fluffy clouds as soft as a pillow -
I could rest my head on them;
A golden river running molten like the sun
I'd wear a golden crown like all my friends,
Glorious princesses dancing like angels.
Animals would dance around me singing songs.
I'd dance with them and sing.
I'd lift up from the ground and start to fly
Up in the starlit heavens high.
I'd meet with kings and queens who'd give me gold
And jewels like no other riches seen before.
I watch jousting ancient knights of old
And even meet Sir Lancelot and talk.
The ladies of the court would dance with me
Gracefully dancing minuets or quick gavottes.
In castles and palaces I'd free
Prisoners and explore the towers and turrets and chambers,
Galleries and halls.
I'd be a guest at a banquet with mounds
Of fruit, meat and ruby wine.
I'd look at portraits in the gallery
And hope to find a portrait of me.

Rebecca Sparks (12)

PEACE ON EARTH

If only there was peace on Earth,
Complete and utter sanctuary,
No more quarrels and angry hearts,
Where everyone is very merry.

Where children laugh and play together,
And great world leaders never fight,
Where grenades and bombs don't fly around,
Disturbing such a peaceful night.

You'd never be afraid to stop outside,
And wander round all day,
Never nervously darting your eyes,
In case you're someone's prey.
Everyone would join together,
English, African and Dutch,
Do you think that this could happen
Or am I wishing for just too much?

Hannah Jones (11)

IF ONLY

If only the world was pretty and pleasant,
There'd be no crime or pollution,
The brown, grotty ocean would be an exotic blue,
Everyone would like this world, animals too.

If only the sound of bullets and bombs had never been heard before,
If accidents were extinct and robbery didn't happen.
There'd be no worry or war.

If only volcanoes, tornadoes and avalanches did not destroy,
If people were fit and healthy,
And nobody was killed or hurt.
Children were always happy, not bullied or abused,
The world would be such a better place,
And nobody would lose.

Our world would be a happy place,
Devastation far away,
Everyone would enjoy their life,
Including you and me.

Rachel Cook (12)

GETTING ON

I'm wishing for eternal youth,
because I'm slowly getting old.
But only for my aching body,
'Cos my mind is stuck on hold.

I'm only twenty-one,
Born the first of February,
In nineteen fifty-nine.

It'll take one hundred years,
before I reach twenty-two,
in my forever young mind.

Danny Coleman

WISHING

After seeing starving people on TV,
I wish they could all live with me.
I wish, when playing with my dolls,
inspired and in happy family mood,
I could give to starving children,
all my imaginary family's food.

I wish a banquet would drop,
from the sky.
So my TV wouldn't show me
how starving people die.

I wish all the food being wasted,
could on the tongues,
of starving people be tasted.
So they wouldn't have to die
withered and wasted.

I wish because wishing is all I can do.

Mandy Ann Cole

GO AWAY WISH

Wish I could be famous, drive a big car,
travel by jet aeroplane, to places afar.
See every country's beautiful creatures,
be appreciative of man-made features.
Take in all the magic, of every land,
give everyone in need, a helping hand.

Wish I could, stop suffering and pain,
help war-torn countries start again.
Make life easier for the poorest of poor,
leave presents of food outside their door.
Make Santa Claus work every day,
so I don't have to wish
the bad world would go away.

Andy Monnacle

MY WISH

I wished the stars were blinding lights
I wished there were no wars or fights
I wished I could paint the sky
While the birds were all flying by
I wished I had a flying horse
I wished to call it Inspector Morse
I wished I could fly around
I wished it wasn't boring on the ground
Then week by week
Nothing was bleak
As all my wishes came true
It was all straight out of the blue
And the stars were blinding lights
There were no wars there were no fights
I could paint the sky
While birds flew by
I had a flying horse
Called Inspector Morse
I could fly around
And it wasn't boring on the ground
And so I was very happy.

Helen Sankey (9)

I WANT TO CHANGE MY NAME

I want to change my name.
I don't like my name.
It could be fame if I change my name.

But my mum said *'No.'*
I said I will break my toe,
But she said *'No.'*

And my dad said *'No.'*
I said I will cover him with dough,
But he said *'No.'*

I asked my sister if she had a name I could have,
But she said *'No way'*
I said I would be her slave for a day.

So I was her slave for a day.
She said to me dance around and say 'Nay.'
I said 'OK.'

so at the end of the day she said 'OK.'
She said 'The name for you will be
Emily May.'

Patrick Hopson (9)

My Mother's Wish

My brother and me, oh how we do fight,
My mother she shouts, 'Get out of my sight!'
We squabble and tumble all over the floor,
My mother shouts loud, then she slams the door.
Oh how she wishes for peace and good will
Between us both, 'oh try not to kill'.
Oh she wishes for love and care
'Please don't chuck her right down the stairs.'
We try to stop bickering as we think we should.
Then all hell breaks loose. Mom knew that it would.
Then peace comes. Why? I haven't a clue,
My mother is happy. Her wish has come true.
We love each other really. My mum knows we do,
That's why she is so happy but just wait a day or two!

Jennifer Laity (9)

GRANDMA IN SPACE

One day Grandma wanted to go to space.
Her grandchildren said 'We'll put rocket boosters on you,
And catch fire to them.'

So on the weekend night,
Ben her grandson,
Pushed her outside to the garden,
And they put the rocket boosters on,
And they caught fire to them,
And she whizzed off.
Her dream had finally come true.

Malcolm Hearn (8)

I Wish I Wish I Wish

I made a wish
And it was for a fish,
That came in a doggy dish,
The fish died and ended up with chips, salt and vinegar,
Then I ate my lovely fish,
Out of the doggy dish.
Then one night my wish came true,
And it was out of the blue.

Charlie Palmer (9)

MY WISH

I wish for a flying dog
And I wish it can see in the fog.
I wish it has silver feet
And I wish it can eat meat.

I wish it can stick labels
And I wish it can read fables.
I will ride it in every race
And I will name it 'Face.'

I wish it is funny
And I wish it has some money.
It came true
And it went 'Moo!'

Luke Curtis (8)

MY WISH

My friend and I made a wish
You would probably think it was to get a fish!
What I really wished for was a magic pig.
Instead I got a magic wig!
So what I did with the magic wig was . . .
Turned it into a magic pig!

Demelza Hambrook-Nute (9)

I Want A Dog To Train

I wanted a dog to train
I asked my dad he said 'No.'
I thought it was a good idea
My sister said 'No.'
So I left them alone.

Next
I asked my nan
If I could train Heidi
She said 'Yes,' so I went mad,
And leapt round the room.

'Come on Heidi.'
I gave her a treat.
I said 'I love you'.
My wish had come true.

Victoria Sarah Triggs (8)

I WISH, I WISH, I WISH

I wish I could paint the moon.
I wish the stars were as bright as fires.
I wish the sky was as colourful as a rainbow.
I wish the sun was out in the winter like a summer's day.
I wish a flying pig would come along,
Pick me up and take me away.
I wish that bright twinkling star was out
And would grant my wish for this day.
Darkness fell and the bright stars were out.
My dream came true out of the blue.
I did everything that I wanted to do.

Christie Smith (9)

A WISH COME TRUE

Oh I wish I had a fish
With a tank that looks like a dish
Said Danny,
Danny had no pets
But he had lots of nets
That night he wished
For a fish with a tank like a dish
So he did a big wish
The very next day he had a fish
That had a tank like a dish!

Jack Maddern (9)

BLACK BEAUTY

I wished for a horse
I wanted to ride
I like to race
I like to win

I got a horse
It was black
I raced my horse
I won the race.

Brian Pengelly (8)

INJECTION

A flash of silver
A liquid sucked out of a jar
Something coming my way.
I sit there,
Petrified,
Unable to move.
I wish I could run!
The needle sinks deep into my flesh . . .
I hate injections!

Matthew Metcalfe (8)

FEELINGS

Feelings can hurt,
Feelings can cry,
Feelings can soothe you,
Make you, and move you.

Feelings may bring love,
Feelings may bring sorrow.
But whatever they bring you
There's always tomorrow.

Maybe you should stop and think
About all your feelings,
Breathe before you take each step and
Try to find their meanings.

Joseph Devalle (11)

THE ROBIN

Perched on a small fence
Singing a loud, cheerful song.
'I live here. Keep out!'

Nicholas Heijbroek (9)

THE STORM

Lightning flashes
Thunder crashes
Grey clouds boil
Trees thrash about
Needle sharp rain stabs down
The rain starts to calm
The lightning stops
The thunder crashes one last time
Then . . .
      Silence.

Angela Hicks (9)

PENGUIN

Plodding slowly
Down the smooth, cold ice
Swoosh! He slithers into the water
White tummy gleams
Twisting and turning
Through the ice-blue water.

Thomas Gray (10)

SLOTH

Always hanging round
Upside down in trees
Enjoying doing absolutely nothing . . .
What a boring life he leads
Up there.

Matthew Howcroft (9)

ELEPHANTS

Strolling in the jungle
Their tough, grey, wrinkled skin like leather
Tusks like swords
Trunks like hosepipes
Reaching up to grab the leaves.

Charlotte Dowding (9)

CAT

Quietly
Through the long grass he crawls
Looking for mice
Tail swishing slowly
Ears twitching
He waits.

Jessie Clarke (9)

MY WISH WOULD BE . . .

If I had a wish it would be
To go on holiday to Benidorm.
Mum and Ches would come too.
There'd be a big square pool
And we'd swim every day.
We'd play each hour away
Before visiting the screen
Whilst eating ice-cream.
Then it's off to the disco
Or watch a pantomime show.
Exhausted.
'To bed' Mum said 'sweet dreams.'

Tim Gardner (11)

WHAT IS YOUR WISH?

I wish I was famous and a millionaire
Why? To buy everything
I wish my family had enough money to go on holiday
Why? They deserve the best!
I wish our school to have more equipment
Why? So we can learn more
I wish the country would be thoughtful and think about poor,
$$\text{poor people}$$
Why? So they can live
I wish the world would stop all the wars - now!
Why? So people won't get hurt!
I wish the planet a long and happy future
Why? So we can all enjoy its rich treasures.

Jarrod Edge (7)

WISHFUL THINKING

Remote control chair
Own money machine
Teddies telling jokes
Floating on a cloud
Everlasting sweets
Invisible rubbish
Magic bus
Homework doing robot
Fast healing medicine
Story telling books.

Anon

WISHFUL THINKING

Intelligent talking dogs
Flying scooters
Colourful falling stars
Chocolate swimming pool
Everlasting chocolate bar
Penguins could fly
Pictures come to life
I know everything.

Sarah Atkinson & Sophie Knights

I WISH

I wish I were a robin
I'd get to sing his sweet song
And keep all those listening
Happy all day long!
Such a chirpy feathered friend
With ruddy breast aglow
Warming even the coldest hearts
When the north wind doth blow.
I wish I were a magpie
With his top hat and tails
Ever chattering in the background
At dinner devouring juicy snails.
I wish I were a collared dove
Co-cooing in the loft
Ousing sentiments of love
Sweet, tender and soft.
I wish I were an eagle
Soaring to incredible height
Diving for the family dinner
In waters bubbling bright.

It is not totally absurd
That when last breath, expired.
I could well be a bird, feathered
The Indian soul so fired
Friends in flight - a culture spurned?
My belief, chosen flocks are airborne
Keeping an eagle eye, an over view
Spirit of mankind returned!
Wishes as dreams, often do come true.

D Wilkinson